Vocal Selections From Walt Disney's

Words and Music by
RICHARD M. SHERMAN and ROBERT B. SHERMAN

CONTENTS

ISBN 0-88188-603-3
(previously ISBN 0-89524-184-6)

HAL•LEONARD™
CORPORATION
7777 W. BLUEMOUND RD. P.O. BOX 13819
MILWAUKEE, WISCONSIN 53213

"MARY POPPINS"

Synopsis

Bert, a street entertainer, introduces the residents of Cherry Tree Lane, a curving bit of road in a charming section of London, circa 1910. Among them are the Banks family, whose household is an uproar over the abrupt departure of their nanny, Katie Nanna. This leaves the children, Jane and Michael solely in the hands of their parents, Mr. & Mrs. Banks. However, their mother's time is tied up with important suffragette work and their father is a bank executive with even less time for his family. Ellen, the maid, refuses to take on the added responsibility.

Mr. Banks must place an advertisement in The Times for another nanny, so the children write their own ad requesting that a nanny "must be kind, must be witty, very sweet and very pretty...." Their father, who prefers the solemn, scowly type of nanny, tears their suggested ad into small pieces and burns it in the fireplace.

The next morning, a line of stern-looking women wait in front of the Banks house; at the hour of eight they will be interviewed. The hour is announced by Admiral Boom, the Banks' next door neighbor, and his assistant, Binnacle, as they fire the large cannon atop his house. The chinaware and teacups rattle and clatter with the reverberation, but the Banks family survives the crisis, as it has twice a day since moving to Cherry Tree Lane.

Admiral Boom has noticed a change in the wind; the westwind has faltered and a breeze is coming strongly from the east. Swept in on the eastwind is a young woman. When Mr. Banks orders the door opened to begin the interviews, he finds that all the applicants have vanished, save one. She is Mary Poppins—serene of countenance and sweet of face—and in her hand she clutches the children's ad, supposedly destroyed.

The children are elated. She is just the nanny they had envisioned in their dreams. Mr. Banks is slightly bewildered and less certain of her. Instead of him interviewing her, she interviews him. The next thing he knows she has agreed to accept the Banks family as employers.

continued on page 43

The Perfect Nanny

Words and Music by
RICHARD M. SHERMAN
and ROBERT B. SHERMAN

4

water. If you won't scold and dom-i-nate us,

We will nev-er give you cause to hate us; We won't hide your spec-ta-cles so

you can't see, Put toads in your bed or pep-per in your tea.

JANE and MICHAEL

Hur-ry, Nan-ny! Man-y thanks. Sin-cere-ly, Jane and Mich-ael Banks.

5

Sister Suffragette

Words and Music by
RICHARD M. SHERMAN
and ROBERT B. SHERMAN

We a-gree that as a group they're rath - er stu - pid!

Cast off the shack - les of yes - ter - day! ____

Shoul - der to shoul - der in - to the ____ fray! Our daugh-ters'

daugh-ters will a - dore us, And they'll sing in grate-ful chor - us, "Well

done, Sis - ter Suf - fra - gette!"

From Ken - sing - ton to Bill - ings-gate one

hears the rest - less cries! From ev - 'ry cor - ner of the land:

"Wom-an-kind, a - rise!" Po - lit - i - cal e - qual - i - ty and

e - qual rights with men! ____ Take heart! for Mis - sus Pank-hurst has been
clapped in irons a - gain! ____ No more the meek and mild sub-ser-vi-ants
we! _____ We're fight-ing for our rights, mil - i-tant-
ly! (Nev-er you fear!) So, cast off the shack - les of

yes-ter - day! ___ Shoul-der to shoul - der in-to the ___ fray! Our daugh-ters' daugh-ters will a - dore us, And they'll sing in grate-ful chor - us, "Well done! Well done! Well done, Sis - ter Suf - fra - gette!" ___

A Spoonful Of Sugar

Words and Music by
RICHARD M. SHERMAN
and ROBERT B. SHERMAN

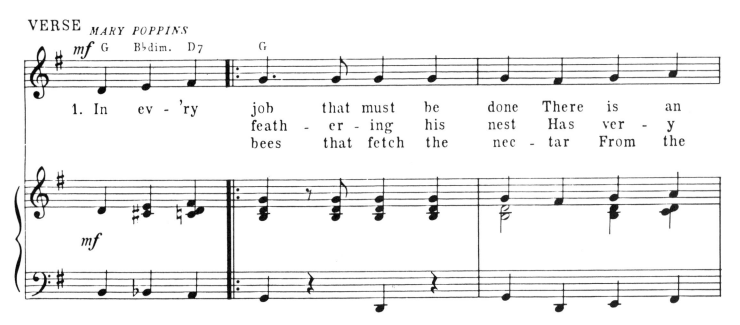

snap! The job's a game; _____ And ev-'ry task you un-der-
bits of twine and twig. _____ Though quite in-tent in his pur-
buzz-ing to and fro _____ Be-cause they take a lit-tle

take Be - comes a piece of cake, A
suit, He has a mer - ry tune to toot; He
nip From ev - 'ry flow - er that they sip, And

lark! A spree! It's ver - y clear to see
knows a song Will move the job a - long,
hence, they find Their task is not a grind,

CHORUS

That a
For a spoon - ful of su - gar helps the med - i - cine go
For a

12

Supercalifragilisticexpialidocious

Words and Music by
RICHARD M. SHERMAN
and ROBERT B. SHERMAN

loud e - nough, you'll al - ways sound pre - co - cious. Sup - er - cal - i -

frag - il - is - tic - ex - pi - al - i - do - cious! Um did - dle did - dle did - dle,

um did - dle ay! Um did - dle did - dle did - dle, um did - dle ay!

cause I was a - fraid to speak When I was just a
trav - eled all a - round the world And ev - 'ry - where he
when the cat has got your tongue, There's no need for dis -

BERT Be -
MARY POPPINS { He
So

lad, Me fa - ther gave me nose a tweak And told me I was bad. But
went He'd use his word and all would say, "There goes a clev - er gent!" (When
may. Just sum - mon up this word And then you've got a lot to say. *BERT* (But

then one day I learned a word That saved me ach - in' nose, *BERT and MARY POPPINS* The
dukes and ma - 'a - ra - jas Pass the time of day with me, I
bet - ter use it care - ful - ly Or it can change your life. *PEARLIE* One

big - gest word you ev - er 'eard And this is 'ow it goes: Oh!
say me spe - cial word And then they ask me out to tea. *ALL* Oh!
night I said it to me girl And now me girl's me wife. *ALL* She's

CHORUS

1.& 2. Sup - er - cal - i - frag - il - is - tic - ex - pi - al - i - do - cious!
3. Sup - er - cal - i - frag - il - is - tic - ex - pi - al - i - do - cious!

Stay Awake

Words and Music by
RICHARD M. SHERMAN
and ROBERT B. SHERMAN

Though the world is fast a-sleep, Though your pil-low's soft and deep, You're not sleep-y as you seem, Stay a-wake, don't nod and dream; Stay a-wake, don't nod and dream.

Jolly Holiday

Words and Music by
RICHARD M. SHERMAN
and ROBERT B. SHERMAN

Lyrics:

1st time *BERT*
2nd time *MARY POPPINS*

Ain't it a glo-ri-ous day?
Now then, what-'d be nice? We'll

Right as a morn-in' in May. I feel like I could fly.
start with rasp-ber-ry ice, And then some cakes and tea.

'Ave you ev-er seen the grass so green, Or a blu-er sky?___ Oh,
Or-der what you will, there'll be no bill, It's com-pli-men-ta - ry.___ Oh,

CHORUS

it's a jol - ly 'ol - i - day with Ma - ry.   Ma - ry makes your 'eart so
it's a jol - ly hol - i - day with you, Bert.   Gen - tle - men like you are

light!   When the day is gray and or - di - nar - y,
few.   Though you're just a dia - mond in the rough, Bert,

Ma - ry makes the sun shine bright! ___   Oh,   'ap - pi - ness is bloom-in' all a -
Un - der - neath, your blood is blue! ___   You'd   nev - er think of press-ing your ad -

round 'er.   The daf - fo - dils are smil - in' at the dove. ___   When
van - tage.   For - bear - ance is the hall - mark of your creed. ___   A

PATTER CHORUS: *Spoken to 1st twelve measures of chorus while piano plays chords on first and third*
BERT: *beats of each measure. Resume singing at * .*

Mavis and Sybil 'ave ways that are winning
And Prudence and Gwendolyn set your 'eart spinning;
Phoebe's delightful, Maude is disarming,
Janice, Felicia, Lydia, charming;
Winifred's dashing, Vivian's sweet,
Stephanie's smashing, Priscilla a treat;
Veronica, Millicent, Agnes and Jane,
Convivial company, time and again;
Dorcas and Phyllis and Glynis are sorts,
I'll agree are three jolly good sports,
But cream of the crop, tip of the top,
It's Mary Poppins, and there I stop!

I Love To Laugh

23

INTERLUDE

mf C *MARY POPPINS*

teeth, good-ness sakes, Hiss-ing and fizz-ing like snakes. (Tzz tzz

tzz.) Some laugh too fast, *(rapid staccato laugh)* some on-ly

blast, (Hah!) Oth-ers, they twit-ter like birds. (Tee hee hee hee

hee!) Then there's the kind that can't make up their mind:

Chim Chim Cher-ee

Words and Music by
RICHARD M. SHERMAN
and **ROBERT B. SHERMAN**

CHORUS

Chim chim-in-ey, chim chim-in-ey, chim chim cher-ee! A sweep is as luck-y, as luck-y can be. Chim chim-in-ey, chim chim-in-ey, chim chim cher-oo! Good luck will rub off when I shakes 'ands with

you, Or blow me a kiss and that's luck-y, too.

VERSE

Now, as the lad-der of
I choose me bris-tles with

life 'as been strung, You may think a sweep's on the bot-tom-most
pride, yes, I do: A broom for the shaft and a brush for the

rung. Though I spends me time in the ash-es and smoke, In
flue. Though I'm cov-ered with soot from me 'ead to me toes, A

this 'ole wide world there's no 'ap - pi - er bloke.
sweep knows 'e's wel - come wher - ev - er 'e goes.

Up where the smoke is all bill - ered and curled, 'Tween pave - ment and

stars, is the chim - ney sweep world. When there's 'ard - ly no day nor

'ard - ly no night, There's things 'alf in shad - ow and 'alf - way in

light, On the roof-tops of Lon-don, coo, what a sight!

Tempo I

Chim chim-in-ey, chim chim-in-ey, chim chim cher-ee! When

you're with a sweep you're in glad com-pa-ny.

No-where is there a more 'ap-pi-er crew Than

them wot sings, "Chim chim cher - ee, chim cher - oo!"

Chim chim - in - ey, chim chim, cher - ee, chim cher - oo!

Chim Chim Cher-ee

PROLOGUE VERSION

Room 'ere for everyone, gather around;
The constable's responsable! Now, 'ow does that sound?
Ullo, Miss Lark, I've got one for you:
Miss Lark loves to "wark" in the park with Andrew!
Ah, Missus Corey, a story for you:
Your daughters were shorter than you, but they grew!
Dear Miss Persimmon, — (pause) — winds in the east — there's a mist coming in,
Like something is brewing and 'bout to begin.
Can't put my finger on what lies in store,
But I feel what's to 'appen all 'appened before.

THE "SIDEWALK ARTIST" VERSION

Chim chiminey, chim chimney, chim chim cheroo!
I does what I likes and I likes what I do.
Today I'm a screever and as you can see,
A screever's an artist of 'ighest degree.
And it's all me own work from me own memory.
Chim chiminey, chim chimney, chim chim cheroo!
I drawers what I likes and I likes what I drew.
No remuneration do I ask of you,
But me cap would be glad of a copper or two,
Me cap would be glad of a copper or two.

Step In Time

Words and Music by
RICHARD M. SHERMAN
and ROBERT B. SHERMAN

NOTE: Additional verses could be improvised by participant. Example: 1. Under the table, step in time! 2: Clap your hands, step in time!

Feed The Birds (Tuppence A Bag)

Words and Music by
RICHARD M. SHERMAN
and ROBERT B. SHERMAN

Come feed the lit-tle birds, show them you care And you'll be
glad if you do; _____ Their young ones are hun-gry, their
nests are so bare; All it takes is tup-pence from you. _____

CHORUS

Feed _____ the birds, tup-pence _____ a bag, Tup-pence, _____

tup-pence, ____ tup-pence ____ a bag. Feed ____ the birds," (If only chorus is sung) the

that's what she cries, While o - ver - head, her birds fill the
bird wom - an

Slightly faster

skies. All a - round the ca - the - dral the saints and a - pos - tles Look

down as she sells her wares. _____ Al - though you can't

see it, you know they are smil-ing Each time some-one shows that he cares. Though her words are sim-ple and few, Lis-ten, lis-ten, she's call-ing to you: "Feed the birds, tup-pence a bag, Tup-pence, tup-pence, tup-pence a bag."

Let's Go Fly A Kite

Words and Music by
RICHARD M. SHERMAN
and ROBERT B. SHERMAN

CHORUS

string of your kite.
string of your kite.

Oh! _____

Let's go fly a kite Up to the high - est height! Let's go fly a kite And send it soar -